208149

DEADLY SPIDERS

PowerKiDS
press™
New York

Published in 2008 by The Rosen Publishing Group, Inc.
29 East 21st Street, New York, NY 10010

First Edition

Editor: Jennifer Way
Book Design: Kate Laczynski
Photo Researcher: Nicole Pristash

Photo Credits: Cover, pp. 1, 5, 7, 9, 11, 13, 15 © Shutterstock.com; p. 17 © Buddy Mays/Getty Images; p. 19 © Rob and Ann Simpson/Getty Images; p. 21 (main) © SuperStock, Inc.; p. 21 (inset) © Getty Images.

Library of Congress Cataloging-in-Publication Data

McFee, Shane.
   Deadly spiders / Shane McFee. — 1st ed.
      p. cm. — (Poison!)
   Includes index.
   ISBN-13: 978-1-4042-3795-7 (library binding)
   ISBN-10: 1-4042-3795-X (library binding)
   1. Spiders—Juvenile literature. I. Title.
   QL458.4.M425 2008
   595.4'4—dc22
                                          2006101501

Manufactured in the United States of America

CONTENTS

SPIDERS !

Are you afraid of spiders? Many people are. Most spiders will not hurt you. Some are even helpful. They eat small pests, like flies and cockroaches.

All spiders are **predators**. This means they prey, or feed, on other animals. Spiders eat small animals like bugs.

There are more than 40,000 **species** of spiders in the world. Only about 200 of these species can hurt people.

Do you want to know more about spiders? Do you want to learn about spiders that are dangerous?

This book will teach you about these creepy creatures' world.

This is a close-up of a common house spider sitting in its web. Even though it looks scary, this kind of spider will not hurt you.

SPIDERS ARE NOT INSECTS

People sometimes mistake spiders for **insects**. Spiders might look a little like insects, but they are **arachnids**. How can you tell arachnids from insects? Arachnids have eight legs and two main body parts. Scorpions, ticks, and mites are also arachnids.

Most species of spiders have eight eyes. This does not mean they can see that well, though. Most spiders can make out only light and dark. The main way spiders sense the world around them is through the tiny hairs on their legs. These hairs allow spiders to smell, hear, and sense **vibrations**.

Look closely at this spider's legs. You can see the tiny hairs that help the spider take in its surroundings.

STicKY TRAPS

Spiders use **spinnerets** to make the silk that they use to build webs. The spinnerets look like tiny arms on the spider's **abdomen**. Most spiders have six.

Different species make different kinds of webs. The most common webs are called orb webs. These look like spirals. Some spiders make funnel-shaped webs. Other spiders make messy-looking, tangled webs.

Spiders build their webs so that some threads are sticky while others are not. Prey get stuck on the sticky parts, and the spiders walk on the nonsticky parts to get to their prey. Their sticky webs also help keep spiders safe from birds, wasps, and other predators.

Spiders are the only arachnids that can spin webs. This spider is building an orb web.

DiNNERtIME

How does a spider know that it has trapped an animal? It feels vibrations in the web through the tiny hairs on its legs. The spider then climbs on the web toward the trapped animal.

The spider then bites the animal with its **chelicerae**. These are the teeth near the spider's mouth. Spiders do not chew their food. The spider's chelicerae work like straws. They use them to suck the insides out of the prey's body!

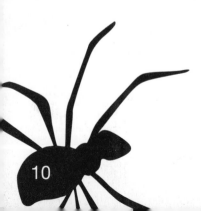

Chelicerae

In this picture, the chelicerae have been labeled. The chelicerae are strong mouthparts that spiders use to suck the guts out of their prey.

SPIDER BITES

A spider's poison is called venom. When a spider bites an animal, the chelicerae **inject** venom.

Different species have different kinds and strengths of venom. Some venoms kill the spider's prey. Other venoms **paralyze** it. Many spiders use their venom to **liquefy** the prey's body parts. This makes it easier for the spider to suck out its prey's insides.

Generally, spiders bite only the animals that they can eat. People are much too big. Most spiders are shy and will run away from people if they can. Spiders will bite people only in **defense**. Most spider bites feel itchy, but bites from some species are dangerous to people.

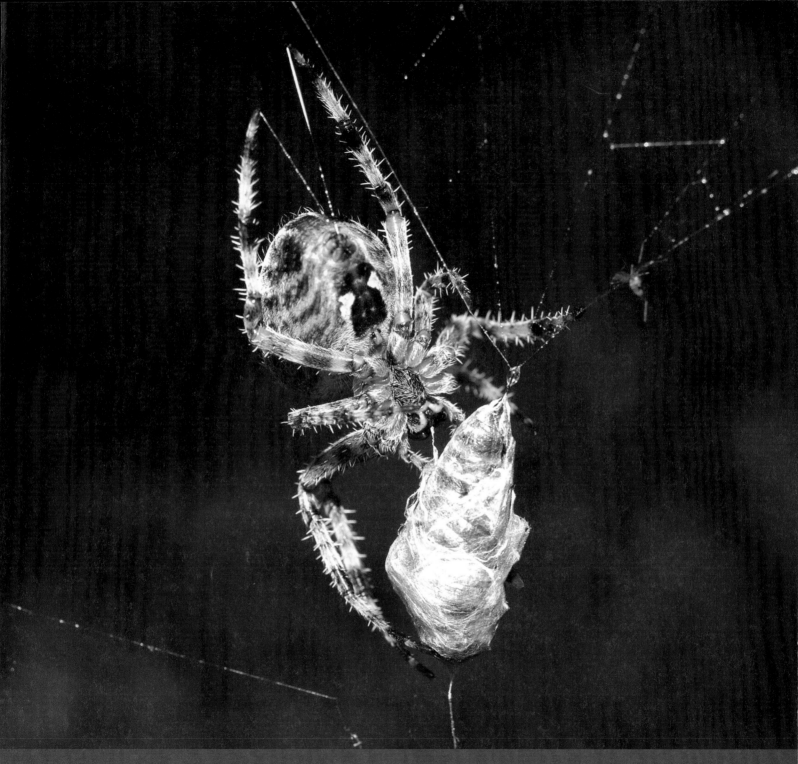

This spider has caught a wasp in its sticky web. It is moving in to kill the wasp and eat it up!

SPIDERLINGS

When spiders **mate**, the male spider **fertilizes** the female. After mating, the female sometimes mistakes the male for prey and eats him!

After mating, the female lays her eggs. Then she spins silk to create an egg sac around her eggs. Some species can lay hundreds of eggs at a time.

When baby spiders hatch, or come out of their eggs, they are called spiderlings. They grow by **molting**. Spiderlings molt many times over a short time. When they have grown enough to live outside the egg sac, spiderlings spin tiny lines of silk to float on the wind. This is called ballooning.

These little spiderlings are newly hatched. Inset: This is what a group of spider eggs looks like when they are inside the egg sac.

THE BLACK WIDOW

The female black widow is one of the most dangerous spiders to people in North America. The male's venom is not dangerous to people.

The female black widows are black and shiny. Sometimes they have small reddish marks that look like hourglasses on their abdomens.

Most people will not die from the black widow female's bite, even though it will be painful. She can kill only small children and people with heart problems.

Many people believe that the females often kill the males after fertilization. This does not happen very often, but it is how the black widow got her name.

The venom of this female black widow is 15 times more powerful than the same amount of venom from a rattlesnake! Luckily, a black widow's bite does not inject as much venom as a rattlesnake's bite.

THE BROWN RECLUSE

The brown recluse is one of the world's most dangerous spiders. It lives in North America in cellars and other dark, quiet places. The brown recluse is small and brown. It has a mark on its abdomen that looks like a violin. It attacks people only when it feels it cannot escape from them.

The venom from a brown recluse's bite can cause a person's skin to rot around where the spider bit. This can grow into a wound as big as a quarter. The bites are painful and take a long time to heal. Like the black widow's bite, the brown recluse's bite is most dangerous to small children and people in poor health.

Brown recluse spiders can be easy to miss in the darkened spaces they like, which can lead to a person getting a painful bite. The word "recluse" means "a person who likes to be alone."

THE SYDNEY FUNNEL-WEB SPIDER

Many people believe that the Sydney funnel-web spider is the most dangerous spider in the world. It lives in Australia and is named after the Australian city of Sydney. The Sydney funnel-web spider mostly eats insects, but sometimes it kills bigger animals, such as frogs.

Sydney funnel-web spiders can be either brown or black. They are known for having chelicerae strong enough to bite through people's shoes!

Male funnel-web spiders are more aggressive, or ready to fight, than the females. Most people bitten by the Sydney funnel-web spider will die unless they see a doctor.

Chelicerae

The Sydney funnel-web spider's bite can kill a person in under 2 hours if left untreated. Inset: This is a close-up of the Sydney funnel-web spider's strong chelicerae.

LEAVE THEM ALONE !

Most spiders are harmless. They are much more afraid of you than you are of them and will try to get away from you if they can.

If you think you have been bitten by one of the dangerous spiders, call the Poison Control Center at 800-222-1222. You should also see a doctor. Doctors have drugs that treat spider bites. These drugs are called **antivenoms**.

If you see a spider in your home, do not panic. Remember, spiders are also helpful creatures that eat flies, cockroaches, and other yucky pests.

GLOSSARY

abdomen (AB-duh-mun) The large, rear part of an arachnid's body.

antivenoms (an-tee-VEN-umz) Drugs that treat bites from venomous animals.

arachnids (uh-RAK-nidz) Types of animals. Spiders and ticks are arachnids.

chelicerae (kih-LIH-seh-ree) A spider's mouthparts.

defense (dih-FENS) Something a living thing does that helps keep it safe.

fertilizes (FUR-tuh-lyz-ez) Puts male cells inside an egg to make babies.

inject (in-JEKT) To force something into a body.

insects (IN-sekts) Small creatures that often have six legs and wings.

liquefy (LIH-kwuh-fy) To turn something hard into something that flows.

mate (MAYT) To join together to make babies.

molting (MOHLT-ing) Shedding hair, feathers, shell, or skin.

paralyze (PER-uh-lyz) To take away feeling or movement.

predators (PREH-duh-terz) Animals that kill other animals for food.

species (SPEE-sheez) One kind of living thing. All people are one species.

spinnerets (spih-nuh-RETS) Parts, located on the rear of the spider's body, that make silk.

vibrations (vy-BRAY-shunz) Fast movements up and down or back and forth.

INDEX

WEB SITES

Due to the changing nature of Internet links, PowerKids Press has developed an online list of Web sites related to the subject of this book. This site is updated regularly. Please use this link to access the list: www.powerkidslinks.com/poi/dspid/